Tuning in to your power
feels like journeying
an entire lifetime
only to awaken one day
and find that you are
less mortal, *more god*
less human, *more spirit*
a far cry away from
the woman you grew up
believing yourself to be
you are an alchemist
of light and energy
creating in every breath
living outside the bounds
of established limitations
and between the veil
of what is manifesting
and what has manifested.

contents

AN INTRODUCTION TO THE ART OF MANIFESTATION

A GUIDED MANIFESTATION JOURNAL

She Manifests More

AN INTRODUCTION TO THE ART OF MANIFESTATION

Affirm: I am the creator and author of my story. When I am aligned, I can attract anything I desire into my life, be it to the good of all and harm of none.

An Intro to Manifestation

Manifestation is the art of intuitive and intentional creation. It is the language of the Universe, the mechanism by which the world as we know it came to exist. This ancient art is depicted in the first book of the Bible, The Book of Genesis. In Genesis 1:3, it says, "And God *said* let there be light, and there was light." From the very beginning God was teaching us to create with our words. In The Book of Romans, we're encouraged to speak those things that are not as though they were.

Not only do our spoken words have the power to create, but we are also creating all the time through thought, which is the language of the mind so to speak. As we begin our journey into the art of manifestation, it is important to understand that word and thought work in tandem to pave the path we experience. With deliberate and consistent effort on your behalf, you may bring something into physical form which did not exist at all (or exist in your immediate reality).

The Forces At Work: Your Conscious & Subconscious Mind

Considering that thought plays such a major role in manifestation, let's pause here to break down how it comes into play. There are two types of thought that I'd like to highlight: conscious thought and subconscious thought.

Your conscious mind, considered the masculine part of your mind, collects, sorts and processes information. It decides what to pass on to the subconscious, or feminine part of your mind, based on your dominant experience. Therefore, your most repetitive thoughts and feelings will be directed to your subconscious, which will then act accordingly to draw more energetically resonant experiences to you.

Your subconscious, on the other hand, handles all the processes in your body that you don't have to think about in order to perform. Examples of this would be breathing, swallowing, pumping blood through your body, blinking, and walking. You can perform each of these activities without conscious thought.

Your subconscious is like an undercurrent coursing through you that is always working in the background. As it receives input from the conscious mind, it creates a blueprint in the realm of the unseen. Once a blueprint has been formed in this realm, the next logical step is reflection into the physical.

Can Manifestation Exist Alongside Religion?

The answer is yes, though manifestation is not an art contained within any one religion or spiritual practice.

I encounter people all the time who believe that manifestation refutes their own religious background. Others consider it too far-fetched to reconcile with their perception of the world. What throws many for a loop is the language used. For instance, one may question why God is frequently interchanged with terminology like the Universe, Our Creator, The Most High, The Divine, and so on. I wouldn't let this confuse you. Different people identify with different names and even gender when referencing the Supreme Source from which all life flows. Throughout this journal you will see that I reference God by many names, yet no matter what term is being used, I am ultimately recognizing one Supreme life force - the beginning and end of everything that we know.

Whatever moniker you choose is a personal choice. What truly matters is your recognition that a Supreme Intelligence does exist. Taken just a bit further, you should also understand that this life force energy exists within you, your friends, your family and everyone you encounter.

It is the connecting thread that binds us all together across ethnicities, gender identifications, sexual orientations, socioeconomic classes, and any other demographic that you can possibly name.

Who Is Manifesting For?

Those who want to take creative agency over their lives

We've been hearing these sayings since we were children:

You can be anything you want!

If you can see it, then you can achieve it!

The sky's the limit!

As children, positive affirmations of our potential come in many forms from many people we encounter in our lives. While we hear them spoken quite frequently, what we do not often hear as children is people explaining why these fundamental thought patterns are key to our success. They also do not explain that these thought patterns do not just apply to us as children, but they are tools we can (and should) make use of throughout our lives. As we grow into adults, these are building blocks that we'll need to revisit religiously to remind us of who we are and what we are capable of creating.

In his book, *The Power of Your Subconscious Mind*, Dr. Joseph Murphy says, "Within your subconscious depths lie infinite wisdom, infinite power and infinite supply of all that is necessary, which is waiting for development and expression."

Take a moment to sit with this...

Within your subconscious mind there exists unlimited potential available to you in every moment. Whether you are aware of this power or not, you are creating a physical manifestation of your internal thoughts all the time.

Each of us is an artist, brush in hand, with a canvas before us that we have full creative control over. It takes consistent effort to be aware of this power and as we begin to cultivate our understanding of it we open to its fullness. Make no mistake, we are created in the likeness of that from which we extended. This means that the same creative abilities of our Creator also lie within us!

Those who want to live a life beyond limitation

The power of the subconscious mind can give humans what seem to be superhuman abilities, which allow us to transcend limitations, obstacles and circumstances. However, we may fail to utilize this superpower when addressing our problems. When we experience setbacks on this physical plane, our likely approach is to respond in some physical manner. For example, if we experience an illness we resort to physical therapy, medicine, surgery or some combination of the three. If we experience a shortage of money, we work harder in the pursuit of earning more. If we experience a disagreement, our reaction in some cases can brew to the point of a physical response. If we experience a desire to arrive at a certain destination faster, we exert more effort in the hopes that it will bring us quickly to the end goal that we seek. So often we rely on our body to respond to what we are experiencing.

Yet if you believe and harness the power of the mind, you understand that while the body seems like the most effective route of response, the mind can surpass any limitations that the body is bound to encounter. So if anyone wants to live a life that is not confined or even defined by the limitations that present themselves, this person must become a powerful wielder of the potential that exists within the mind.

What might some of the experiences above look like if we substituted our reliance on physical power with mental power? We might discover our ability to heal our bodies in miraculous ways through thought paired with treatment or in some cases, thought alone. We might realize that our ability to attract greater financial stability is a matter of resonance, which must be achieved by first aligning our thoughts with our desired outcome.

In matters of disagreement, we would provide ourselves with space to process and understand before reacting. Lastly, when we experience contrast between our current reality and what we desire, we'd find ways to live in gratitude and not be so consumed by our impatience that we prolong the actualization.

Those who would like to heal themselves or others

So often we place power outside ourselves, when the power within us is the strongest of all. What exists within each of us is "God power" for our Creator formed us as extensions of His own grace and light. He gave us access to an abundant source of wisdom.

Time and space are of no consequence to Him so He moves and exists freely as an infinite substance flowing through us all. This is an inner intelligence that we are all capable of calling on and working with. We only have to train our minds so that this can happen.

In the book of Mark 11:24, we are given the blueprint to successfully actualizing: "Truly I tell you, if anyone says to this mountain, 'Go, throw yourself into the sea,' and does not doubt in their heart but believes that what they say will happen, it will be done for them." The key to our wildest desires coming into physical form is extreme, unwavering belief despite what our environment, friends, or current challenges may have us believe. Many mistakenly believe that healing and miracles are works of the past or even a select few, but this is not true. Miracles are works that we can each perform once we learn to access the power that resides within. Before we can begin to tap into that power, we have to truly believe that it is available to us.

Principles of Manifestation

The Law of Attraction

The Law of Attraction is a universal truth that says "Like attracts like."

It is important to note that The Law of Attraction acts with complete impartiality and precision. In other words, it does not carefully comb through our assortment of thoughts and only choose those that will generate a desirable reality. The Law of Attraction will return to you the vibrational match of the primary thoughts you send out to the Universe.

So the emotions that we consistently emit, whether ideal or not, will call the experiences with the same vibrational frequency back to us as a physical manifestation. This knowledge can help us to be selective about the thoughts we interact with as we begin to better understand that our inner world shapes our outer experience.

As a spiritual being on this human journey, you will encounter low vibrational energy in many forms, but as you move through the world with this knowledge you should become more vigilant of your response.

Not only should you choose your thoughts carefully, but also the words you speak, the company you keep, the conversations in which you participate, and the environments in which you enter. You must become more aware of the ways you interact with the outer world, because ultimately that will impact what you experience internally. All of these factors are contributing to how you feel emotionally and thus, what you will attract physically.

You may be wondering how it is possible to monitor ourselves and ensure that we are in a high vibrational state of receiving? You can do this by checking in regularly with how you are feeling. How you feel is your window into your vibrational state. You can use a tool like the emotional guidance scale, which we'll discuss later in this book to gauge where you are and develop a better understanding of how "attractive" you are. To be clear, in this context your attractiveness has nothing to do with your appearance and everything to do with the force by which you draw what you desire into your reality.

Whether you use this tool or another, you must become more in touch with your emotions to identify what you are creating in every moment. Everything you are experiencing right now is a result of your past thoughts and emotions so be sure to choose wisely!

Practice Gratitude

The universe is composed of many reflections that present themselves in the most phenomenal ways when you are aware enough to notice. It is one continuous cycle of physical (or seen) imitating the spiritual (or unseen). Considering this, I want you to think of how you feel when someone expresses gratitude to you for something you have done for them. Naturally, it makes you feel good and will likely lead you to do something nice for this person in the future. I don't think anyone will argue with the idea that humans like to feel appreciated.

Might this be an attribute inherited from our greater spiritual origin? Is it possible that our Creator might also enjoy the feeling of being appreciated and feel inspired to give us more when we express our gratitude? I believe so. God wants to give us all the desires of our heart, but like us, it delights Him to be acknowledged for His work in our lives.

When you are appreciative of what you already have, this energy invites more of the same experiences into your life. This is why gratitude is the ultimate emotion to manifest from. There are many ways to incorporate a gratitude practice into your life. Some find it helpful to keep a journal. I personally enjoy keeping a gratitude jar on a nightstand in my room because I know that I will see it many times in the course of a day. This helps me reinforce my practice and remember to add daily reasons for gratitude to this jar.

Find your own way to build a gratitude practice into your daily life that feels good to you!

Specificity is key

Have you ever asked for something only to get what you thought you wanted and realize – whoops, I left some important details out! For a long time, I was focused on manifesting work that I could do from anywhere in the world. At the time, I wasn't so focused on what the work was, how long it took me to do it, or even whether I enjoyed it. I just wanted to be able to get my work done and not have my environment controlled while doing it. After manifesting just that, I realized that I didn't just want any old job. I wanted one that challenged and excited me. I wanted to do work that felt rewarding, like I was contributing to something bigger than myself. It took some more living and learning for me to come to that conclusion.

Often it takes experience to develop a more detailed idea of what we do want and that's okay. Start with what you do know and you can always refine over time. Don't be afraid to dive deep into the details. Examine what you're asking for from every angle and think about how a particular manifestation connects to other aspects of your life. The more you can understand and truly get a feel for what the experience will be like, the more likely you will be happy with the end result.

Meet God halfway

The book "Think & Grow Rich" opens with a story about a man named Edward C. Barnes. Perhaps you know who he is. Barnes had a burning desire to go into business with who we now know as the inventor of the light bulb, Thomas Edison. With this thought at the forefront of his mind, he intentionally took action and caught a freight train to meet Edison (without an appointment) in Orange, New Jersey.

Barnes had no confirmation that his efforts would be successful, but he had conviction in his ability to turn his thoughts into reality. This caused him to move with a level of confidence in the midst of the unknown.

So what does it look like meeting God halfway? Does it look like something so seemingly outlandish as traveling to another state in hopes of having a conversation with a complete stranger? Sometimes, yes, but it may also look like "milder" forms of intentional action. While milder in nature, that does not mean that other forms of action are by any means mild in effect.

For example, if you make the decision to become a well known and celebrated director, there are many ways that you might take intentional action to bridge the gap from your current state to the state at which you hope to arrive. Similar to Barnes, you could hop the next flight to Hollywood and show up at the door of your favorite director's studio. Another option might be for you to enroll in a local film school and begin the process of perfecting the fundamentals.

While the latter option might be considered the less bold of the two, it will still effectively move you closer to your goal. I'd be willing to bet that had Barnes never stepped foot on that train to New Jersey, but kept his burning desire to work with Thomas Edison, paired with some other intentional pursuit of his ultimate goal, that he would have still reached his ideal outcome.

Although God does not need our action to bring our wildest dreams into reality, I believe He waits for proof of our "investment" before giving us what we believe we want. What do I mean by investment? I mean investment of our time, investment of our attention, and investment of our vision. This "divine pause", which can feel a great deal longer on our earthly timeline, is a protective mechanism that helps to weed out our real desires from those that are fleeting.

The ability to be clear and consistent is often the very habit that prevents us from making progress. Our earnesty affirms the degree to which we are invested in the vision we hold. This burning desire, paired with action allows us to work in aligned partnership with the Divine to bring our non-physical desires into physical reality.

Forget about the "how"

I believe that the word "how" can be a single-handed killer of dreams. Think back to when you were a child. You allowed yourself to dream without limitation. The best thing of all is that you believed those dreams without need for explanation as to how they might become your reality.

As you got older, your whimsical, ethereal nature (your subconscious mind) took the backseat to your need for logical answers (your conscious mind). Have you ever taken the time to imagine something really incredible for yourself only to find yourself falling into an endless loop of questions? You become focused on details and convinced that before you can take the first step, you must collect as many of them as you can. You've lost touch of how to navigate without what you believe to be vital pieces of the puzzle. Contrary to what you may have gleaned from mainstream society, your obsession with the "how" will keep you exactly where you are right now, if you aren't careful. You don't need to know the "how". You need only know the "what" (and the "why"). Once you begin to move towards that, all the help you need will show up naturally. This process may feel to many like moving through a dark room, but moving through the darkness is an act of faith!

This darkness that so many are afraid of is a powerful creative environment. Think about the birth of a child. A fetus spends nine months in the darkness of the womb before entering this realm as a new being. In the darkness is where the miraculous happens. During this process of becoming, neither parent nor fetus becomes obsessed with the question of how. As the vessel of a child, a woman trusts that if she nurtures this being, it will grow and eventually enter the world as an infant. She trusts the natural way of things. Manifesting is no different. What you reap is what you sow. It is a natural law so begin to think of it as such.

Steps to Manifest

There are many ways to successfully manifest what you desire. As you journey deeper down this path, you will come across so many unique perspectives. That is a part of what makes this human experience so fascinating, our ability to interpret and process through our own special lens. Below you'll find some techniques and practices that you can use to guide you into this journey.

Feel free to work with what you feel called to and experiment with other techniques you come across. Also, don't be afraid to tap into your own intuitive practices. So many times, we place power outside of ourselves when every answer we need is already within us. Outside practitioners are simply facilitators of your own particular gifts.

You may need to do some excavating to access this knowledge, but you are an old soul, composed of experiences that span across lifetimes. You have access to an infinite supply of information. Once you realize this, you can begin to explore and develop your own tools to receive what is available.

Identify your desires

Ask yourself an honest question. What do you desire? If you ask yourself this question, it is likely that many things will come to mind. Write them all down, however they come, straight from your mind to the paper. Depending on where you are in your journey, you may find yourself drawing a blank when it comes to what you desire for your life.

The best way to cultivate this understanding is simply by living and exposing yourself to new settings, people, hobbies, books, food, and frames of thought – the goal is to give yourself opportunities to deepen your understanding of who you are and what brings you joy.

Exposure develops your interests and preferences, nurturing within you the superpower of specificity. Why do I call specificity a super power? Getting specific seems easy enough, but a great many people find this aspect of manifestation particularly challenging.

Get specific

You have to take a step further from identifying what you want. Many times, when people talk about things they desire, they speak in incredibly broad terms. They may speak about how they want to be happy, how they want to help people around them, or even how they want to spend their time traveling the world. Do you think there is a person on this planet who wouldn't enjoy these things? Of course not. It's human nature to desire enjoyment and pleasure. If this is true, why do so many lives not accurately reflect this known fact?

Most people lack one incredibly important detail when they are speaking about their desires. They are not clear and they are not specific enough. Such "vague and misty" ideas are utterly useless and cannot effectively bring about the reality you seek to actualize.

If you were designing a home, you would never expect that simply telling the builder you want a five bedroom home would give you the home of your dreams. On the contrary, you would come prepared with a long list of tilling choices, backsplashes, light fixtures, structural design plans, paint samples, and so on. There wouldn't be a single detail spared. In the same way, you must get incredibly clear and allow your subconscious to get to work on your plan.

Be consistent

Your daily actions will gradually bring you closer to your vision. It's important to understand that when we refer to actions as they relate to The Law of Attraction, we are referring to any combination of what you think, how you feel and what you do. When you think of your daily actions, consider both a laser and a strobe light.

Both contain light, but a laser is focused while a strobe light is chaotic and sends energy bouncing all over the place. If you bounce around like a strobe light, you will find that it takes you quite a long time (if ever) to see your desires take shape. Energy that resembles a strobe light will confuse the subconscious and result in scattered or sporadic results. You may experience certain aspects of your manifestation, but not see it come to full fruition because your energy is not directed with repetition.

Alternatively, if you can get clear on a specific desire and move in a concerted effort each day toward its realization, like a laser beam, your conscious mind will make a successful impression upon your subconscious mind. Consider this. The more often you perform a certain task, the easier it gets to do until eventually it happens on autopilot without your conscious effort. The more diligently you go after your desires, the more your subconscious takes over to create the physical equivalent of that reality. So in this case, consistency really is key.

Build a vessel

This is such a fun part when it comes to manifestation. You want to create a physical representation of your manifestation that is easy for you to return to again and again as reinforcement. To say that we live in a world of distraction is an extreme understatement. I would go so far as to say that distraction is an intentional agenda because focused minds produce effective results. What benefit would it be to this capitalistic society if everyone were focused, sound and fully attuned with their creative abilities?

People would understand that they can heal themselves. There goes the big pharma industry. People would understand that they can create lasting wealth for themselves. There goes the predatory personal lending industry. People would understand that the power they look for in government, social structures, educational institutions and so on is but a dim light in comparison to the ever-burning fire that dances within them. Poof - just like that, the world as we know it would be completely changed.

The reality is that a shift is already taking place. Now is your time to wake up to your own dormant potential and step completely into it. In the process from inception to actualization, it's important to stay connected with what you are working towards. Below are some examples of how you can consistently relate with your desires:

- *Traditional Vision Board*

Admittedly, this is not my favorite manifestation vessel, but many find success going this route. You can make it a little more aesthetically appealing by creating it within a nice frame instead of the poster boards I've come to despise over the years. What can I say, I'm a stickler for a nice aesthetic in my home and the worst thing to do is create something and hide it in the back of your closet when you're done. You need constant (preferably daily) contact with this object.

- *Digital Vision Board*

This might be my favorite method due to the ease and accessibility. You can use an app like Pinterest to create a board dedicated to your manifestation with pins to support it. You can also use a tool like Canva to create a presentation where you collect and store related images You can be as broad or granular as you choose with either of these approaches, but in my experience, the more detail the better!

- *Manifestation Jar*

Find an empty jar and set it somewhere highly visible. You can write out the details of what you are attracting all at once or periodically over time. Either way, take time to consistently connect with what you have written down as you utilize this creative tool. Everytime you revisit your own words, you carve space for your imaginings to pour forth into reality.

- *Creative Expression*

Explore your artistic side and create your own masterpiece that represents what you are calling in. Connect your pencil or brush to a canvas and bring to life your personal blueprint for the Universe. I know what you're probably thinking – that this is an activity reserved for the artistically inclined. You're absolutely wrong there. Let the feminine lead! While some may bring forth images of an object, an environment, or even a person, you can also evoke your feelings. Imagine the feeling of the effect which has been successfully brought about by the cause

- your thoughts. Allow your creation to be as real or abstract as you desire.

Name your emotions

What will it feel like to successfully manifest? Connecting to that feeling is an integral part of your manifestation journey. These feelings create momentum, a strong current of energy that correlates with the tone of your dominant emotions. If your dominant emotions are those of a lower caliber - emotions like anger, resentment, guilt, hatred, and fear - you will experience momentum into experiences that attract opportunities to feel the way you already feel.

Alternatively, if your dominant emotions are those of a higher caliber - emotions like love, joy, gratitude, excitement, passion, and enthusiasm - you will also experience momentum into experiences that attract opportunities to feel the way you already feel. The only difference is that these feelings will guide you into a future that you desire rather than one that you do not.

What emotions accompany the experience you desire? Name them, examine them, and begin to embody them now. The Universe will continue to mirror whatever experience you choose to commit to.

Emotional Guidance Scale

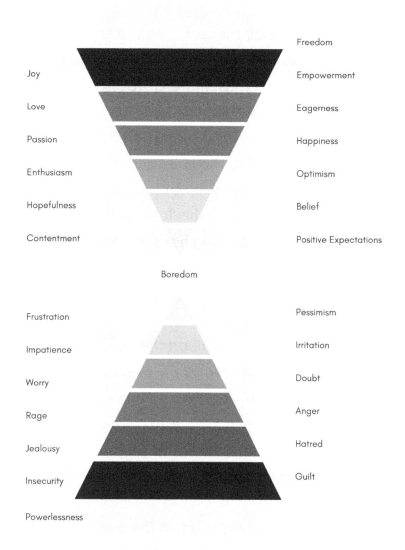

Joy — Freedom / Empowerment

Love — Eagerness

Passion — Happiness

Enthusiasm — Optimism

Hopefulness — Belief

Contentment — Positive Expectations

Boredom

Frustration — Pessimism

Impatience — Irritation

Worry — Doubt

Rage — Anger

Jealousy — Hatred

Insecurity — Guilt

Powerlessness

It can be challenging to give names to some of the feelings that we experience. To help with that assessment and identification, you can utilize a tool like the emotional guidance scale, first introduced by Abraham Hicks. This scale outlines a list of 22 emotions that are indicators of your alignment or lack thereof with the Universe. As you begin to move up this chart vibrationally, you become more connected and thus, more attractive. As you become more acquainted with the emotions you feel, you can gradually reach for the next higher emotion on the scale, making your way up into those emotions that are most powerful in the art of manifestation. Give yourself grace and patience as you begin this journey and don't expect to leap from one end of the scale to another. Take consistent, concerted effort to bring yourself into high vibrational emotions.

Depending on where you fall on the scale, your improvements may not always be evident to those around you, but just remember that each step you take in the direction of better feeling thoughts is a step well taken.

Feel the emotions now

Manifesting can be compared to the concept of a radio. When you tune into a specific station, you will receive the output of that station. As you begin to walk in the feelings your manifestation will bring about, you are actually elevating your own energetic frequency, making it that much easier for you to tune into your desired "station".

Practice feeling these emotions. After all, aren't emotions the most delectable part of any experience? At the core of any human desire is a deeper desire to feel good, simple as that. We want the feeling that comes along with the dream vacation, dream house, or dream car.

As we pursue these various interests, it's important to manifest from a space of contentment and abundance. If you seek material objects in hopes that they will bring about these feelings, you will never be satiated. You will always need something external to keep the emotional "high" going. Alternatively, if you can practice feeling high vibration emotions now, they will eventually become second nature. You'll find that you can feel incredible no matter what circumstances exist around you and that is the purest form of abundance you'll find.

Show up to your glow up

Somewhere in some reality, there is already a version of you that is experiencing what you are currently in the process of calling in. I know this is quite a concept to wrap your mind around, but bear with me and allow your imagination to drive for just a moment here.

If the "future" you is already somewhere swimming in the pool of the multi-million dollar home you're manifesting, might you have an opportunity to connect with this version of yourself? If you do, what kind of insight could you gain from this interaction?

The more you understand about this future version of yourself, the easier it becomes for you to embody the characteristics of this individual. As you begin to walk, talk, dress and think like this person, you begin to close the gap between where (or who) you are now and where (or who) you would like to be.

Harness the power of water

The power of water as an element is unmatched. It is a substance that truly permeates nearly every aspect of our existence.

In our bodies, water trumps food as a necessity for our survival. Without food, we could last two weeks, but without water, we could survive a mere three days. Even still, water is a living substance gravely underestimated in these modern times.

While people understand its obvious abilities to transport,

reshape, nurture, destroy and break down, water's ability to transform in response to its surroundings is not as well known.

Through experiments performed by Dr. Masaru Emoto, water was found to be extremely sensitive to its environment. It can be altered at a molecular level based on what it is exposed to. Hence, the structure of water can tell a story of what energy it has interacted with.

Imagine the potential available in such powerful insight! We can work with these properties of water as an aid in our own manifestation work.

Water Infusion

One way in particular that we can do this is by infusing water with focused energy. I like to start by filling a glass bottle with water. I may hold this bottle while visualizing so that the water is able to bask in the energy and emotions of my experience. I may also speak affirmations into this water regarding a specific manifestation.

You can allow intuition to lead you in this practice. What matters is that as you hold your water vessel, you feel good feelings that will translate into greater alignment with your manifestation. Once you have infused this water, you can utilize it in many ways. You can drink it, use it to cook with, water your houseplants with it, or sprinkle drops of it throughout your home. Consider it your own powerful potion meant to help sustain high vibrations in your day to day experiences.

Another superpower of water that many often fail to acknowledge is its ability to hold information.

Release to water

We can utilize water in our own practices to release energy, emotions, or thoughts that we no longer have use for. If you have access to the ocean, commune with it as often as you can. Recognize that you can trust the ocean to hold what you can no longer carry. The ocean has space and it also has the capacity to neutralize what may have been toxic to you or at the very least, inhibitive.

We get so used to carrying around excessive weight that we don't even recognize the many ways it may be hindering us. Give yourself an opportunity to do an internal scan and take note of the emotions and stories that you have hidden throughout your body. The ones that do not feel good to experience lie behind your slow speed of actualization. You have to give up those stories that are creating resistance in your life.

If you don't have access to the ocean, don't worry! There are other methods of releasing to water. You can incorporate epsom salt or sea salt into your bath or shower routine.

While in the shower or bath, take your salt of choice and rub in a gentle circular motion all over your body. If you notice a slight burning in any areas while you are scrubbing, these may be places where discordant energy has become trapped in your body. Say this affirmation out loud: "I release any stagnant energy that is holding me back."

I can tell you that no matter how much action you believe you are taking in your manifestation journey, this kind of energy build up is interrupting (and prolonging) the process so you must release it.

Visualize during meditation

Visualization offers us a chance to express and exercise our own unique creative faculties. When this power is yielded intentionally, we reconnect to our imagination and work with it to design a reality of our own choosing.

What is so powerful about this practice is that it allows us to return to the ancient knowledge that lives within each of us. We regain awareness of our abilities, our greater (higher) selves, and a spiritual community that exists to assist us in every moment. We remember that there is an infinite substance that permeates every part of the Universe, into and across time, that we can work with to expand the limits of our experience.

As you begin your own visualization practice, you should approach it with one primary objective, to interact with a reality that already exists in the non-physical realm. It's important that you see yourself experiencing this reality. You'll want to connect with the future version of you that is already living out what you are still in the process of manifesting. Develop a relationship with this version of yourself. What does this future version of you look like? How does she dress? What does she spend her time doing? Meet with this version of yourself regularly and be open to what you may learn from this encounter. As you spend more time with this vision, you will build momentum up that causes it to actualize into the physical.

Getting Started With Visualization

There are many ways of practicing visualization. This practice may look different for everyone. It may be something you bring into your meditations, a muscle you build while on a morning walk, or even a skill you marry with other creative activities. Here is an example of how you might introduce visualization into your meditation practice:

1) Cleanse and protect the space you will be utilizing. I really love to use palo santo, but when it is not available, I also use sage. When you are doing any spiritual work, you open up parts of yourself that you may have never accessed during this particular human experience. When you open in these new ways energetically, you may become more tuned into experiences and entities of the non-physical world. This is nothing to be afraid of, but absolutely something of which you should be aware.

2) Sit in a comfortable position and in comfortable clothing with your eyes closed. Focus on your deep inhale and the expansion of your lungs. Then focus on your exhale and contraction of your lungs. Focus on this breath and as thoughts come up, acknowledge them and release them. Sometimes when I'm experiencing a lot of incoming thoughts. I like to imagine them as objects floating around me that I gently set on the ground to address at a later time. It's helpful to have a visual representation for me.

3) Once you have given yourself some time to clear mental space for this activity, you can now begin to focus your attention on a specific event or environment that you are calling in. If you have gone through the process of building a vessel for your manifestation, then you should have a pretty detailed idea of what you are looking to experience. Call on those words and images you put together as you connect with the non-physical representation of your desire. As you begin to incorporate this as a regular practice, you will want to be consistent with these details. Think of it this way, a moving target is more difficult to hit than one that is still. The more consistent and clear you become in this practice, the more still your target becomes.

4) Once you've spent time visualizing the details, you can now focus on connecting to the version of yourself who is living this very experience. You may find it difficult at first to connect with her. If you do, you can try speaking to her in a language that feels comfortable to you. Remember that just like you have access to your angels, guides, and Source energy, you also have the ability to communicate with alternate versions of yourself. You might say something like this: "To the version of me that is experiencing (insert your experience of choice here), I call to you today and ask for your guidance. I ask that you might let yourself be seen and I welcome any advice you

might share to help me bridge the gap from where I am at present to where you are now. Thank you for your loving support and wisdom in this moment and beyond."

5) Always end your visualization practice saying thank you for any spiritual support you have received. If you called on any specific energy to assist you, you can acknowledge that energy and give thanks.

Whatever method you choose, you want to be sure you are connected to your life force energy – your breath. Stay conscious of your inhale and exhale while engaging in any visualization exercise. Think of this as giving life to your vision!

Overtime, your goal with this practice is to move your vision into the present moment. How do you do this? First, you must become aware of your emotions. You can analyze your emotions and use them as a powerful indicator of your degree of alignment or misalignment with Source energy. The more aligned you are with this energy, the better you will feel. The better that you feel, the more receptive you will be. Therefore at the heart of any successful manifestation, is your alignment with God.

Manifestation Methods & Rituals

In support of your manifestation, you can also bring rituals into play. Rituals can be beautiful ways to connect with and emphasize your vision. While there are many ways to do so, you will likely gravitate to one or two that you choose to utilize regularly.

Rituals for abundance involving cinnamon

How is it that cinnamon has come to be affiliated with abundance? Perhaps it has something to do with the fact that this spice, common to the average modern household, was once an expensive and highly coveted commodity, produced mainly in Sri Lanka, formerly known as Ceylon.

For many years, the demand for cinnamon exploded as countries sought its origin and once they found Ceylon, many desired to seize control of it. Portugal was the first to successfully do so and amassed great wealth. Cinnamon was also a major motivation behind the Spanish sailing to and "discovering" America.

So we see the historical significance that cinnamon has, which may be why the spice is now a common ingredient in abundance rituals. Now that access to cinnamon is not so exclusive, we can all take advantage of the magic held by this age-old spice.

If you're looking to invite more abundance into your life - whether it be through better health, greater financial wealth, more loving relationships, or an upgrade in your life experience as a whole, you can use cinnamon to strengthen any internal work you are already doing. I think it's important to say this because if you are not doing the work, it is unlikely that any ritual that you perform will be successful. That being said, here is a cinnamon ritual that you can try:

Items Needed:

- Small to medium-sized muslin or mesh bag
- Cinnamon sticks
- Nutmeg
- Cloves
- Cardamom

Steps:

1. Combine all ingredients inside of your bag of choice.
2. While adding each ingredient repeat this affirmation: "I welcome abundance of all forms into my life. I open myself to receive greater wealth, joy, experiences, and opportunities. May this reality actualize to the good of all and harm of none. And so

it is." While you do not have to say these words exactly, they are just a framework of the energy you want to bring to this ritual.

3. Place your bag inside of your purse or inside of your car to carry with you as you go about your day.

4. Optional: Write your affirmation and place it inside of the bag to better absorb the intention.

Manifesting with salt

Salt has been valued for its many uses for centuries. In fact, if you can imagine, Roman soldiers were once paid with it which is why the word salary has the root of "sal". Salt is also referenced as an item of value throughout the Bible. Considered somewhat of a triple threat, it can be used for cooking food, combatting medical ailments, and cleansing spaces.

Salt has the ability to purify an environment, dispelling any unwanted or stagnant energy. When working with salt, Himalayan salt is ideal since it is the purest form. However, sea salt also works just fine. Stay away from table salt as it has been processed and stripped of many minerals that salt contains naturally which means it is likely stripped of its most powerful properties.

As it relates to manifestation, salt can help you prepare your home and your body for receiving by opening up space. The preparedness of your environment is just as important as your manifestation itself. You can use the following rituals to promote energetic release:

For The Home:

Place containers of your preferred salt in every room of your home to purify energy and counteract any negative influence that may be working against your manifestation.

Set your intention for these salt containers and leave them for 24 hours. Then carry the salt outside of your home to dispose of it. Repeat this ritual when you sense a build up of unsupportive energy in your home.

For The Body:

Run a bath for yourself, adding your preferred salt. You can also add any herbs or oils of your choice whose properties pair well with the intention for your ritual. While you're in the bath, take salt in your hands and rub it in a gentle circular motion over your body's energy centers (i.e your heart, your throat, and sacral chakra). You can also rub it anywhere that you regularly experience tension or pain, as energy build up may be the source of some chronic conditions.

Manifesting before bed

When you think of sleep, you probably think of a time where your body is resting and recuperating. You're right to think so because while you sleep, the conscious part of your mind also rests. On the other hand, your subconscious mind continues working. I like to think of the subconscious mind as a piece of God that resides within us. It is the part of us that brings our deepest and most consistently held desires into fruition.

Once the conscious has successfully impressed an idea onto the subconscious, it must actualize. Sleep represents a door to the subconscious and so the time before bed is prime for manifestation. It's important that we are extremely selective with what we allow to enter our space during this time. We want to be cognizant of the emotional state that we are in as we approach sleep, because our thoughts are like the paints used by our subconscious mind in the work of art that becomes our waking lives.

We can use the time before sleep to regularly reinforce a desired outcome. Each time we do this, we are giving fuel to our subconscious to bring that reality closer.

It makes sense then, to practice some form of visualization before bed. I like to use this time to look at images of something I am currently calling in. For instance, as I write this book, I am in the process of manifesting a new home. One simple way to connect with this reality is to look at photos of this home before bed. I use Pinterest to create vision boards and have one dedicated to the design of this home.

So each night before bed, I like to reinforce that vision and give my subconscious mind something to chew on while I'm in dream land. This is also an ideal time for working with affirmations.

55X5 Manifestation Method

To manifest with the 55x5 method, write down what you are manifesting in the present tense 55 times for five days in a row. The number five is a powerful number which can be a symbol of change and shifts within an individual's life. It also represents freedom, stepping outside of bounds (your current reality), and creative expression (manifestation), which makes it a fantastic number to work with for this ritual.

As you affirm your manifestation through writing, do your best to speak clearly about what you want. Try to focus on the emotions that will accompany the actualization of your desires. It is also very important that your affirmation is written in the present tense because you want to connect with the energy of abundance. If you write your affirmation in a manner that is future-focused, you emphasize the lack in your present reality, inviting more of the same into your experience.

Tips for success

- Opt to handwrite your statements rather than type them on a computer. There is something magical about putting a good old fashioned pen to paper that cannot be recreated with a keyboard.
- Do not multitask while doing this ritual. You want complete focus on the words you are writing so that you have a chance to consciously connect with what you are bringing to life. Your conscious will then impress these statements on your subconscious so it's important that you are fully present while completing this activity.
- This is not a requirement, but try starting this practice at 5:55am or 5:55pm. I prefer morning because it is such a powerful time to connect with the non-physical. During the early morning hours is when the veil separating the physical and spiritual world is the thinnest. When it comes to manifesting, I truly believe that all the desires we are working towards actualizing exist in this alternate reality. Use the

hours before dawn for an extra boost in this ritual.

- If five days feels a little intense for you, try the 33x3 Manifestation Method, which consists of you writing down your affirmation just 33 times every day for three days.

3 6 9 Method

Like the manifestation methods mentioned above, this ritual also involves writing down a statement that embodies what you are in the midst of attracting. The main difference is that you will write this statement at three different intervals throughout your day (rather than at one time, all at once). When you first wake up you will write your manifestation three times, around mid-day you will write your manifestation six times and before bed you will write your manifestation nine times.

The significance of the numbers three, six and nine have been pondered since ancient times. However, the rise in fascination over the years is often attributed to famous inventor, Nicola Tesla, who said that those who understood the power of these numbers had the key to the Universe. Tesla was so intrigued with these numbers, which he believed to be sacred numbers, that he developed rituals related specifically to them. For instance, it is said that Tesla would not enter a building before circling around the block three times. He also refused to stay in any hotel rooms with numbers that were not divisible by three.

When you consider how these numbers relate to our lives, it's easy to see how well integrated they are, particularly three, by which of course, six and nine are divisible.

The number three folds so seamlessly into our reality. It is absolutely everywhere. Our existence consists of three distinct stages: birth, life and death. Matter can occur in three states: solid, liquid and gas. Our experience of time unfolds as a set of three: past, present and future. The basis of Christianity is based upon the Holy Trinity: Father, Son and Holy Spirit. The Hindu story of creation is also connected to the number three, with the deities of Brahma the creator, Vishnu the keeper of reality, and Shiva the destroyer. This concept of a "divine triad" spans across cultures, weaving in and out of history, expressed through art, technology, religion, mythology, and architecture. It's no wonder that these numbers are harnessed in this ritual, bringing us into a deeper connection with the divine.

Tips for success

- Create a manifestation statement that speaks in the present tense and spans 17 seconds when read aloud. It should also start with the word "I" and end in "in my life". For example: I am beyond grateful for my modern 7 bedroom home that allows me to feel deeply rooted in this existence, create lifelong memories with my family and friends, cultivate an abundance of love, and have space to continuously explore new creative curiosities in my life.
- Consider some of your own personal connections to the numbers three, six and nine. How do they show up in your life? How can you further explore that relationship to make this ritual even stronger?

Well Known Present Day Manifesters

Oprah

We can't talk about manifestation without acknowledging one of the most vocal advocates of the law of attraction. Oprah Winfrey is a woman recognized globally as a media mogul, talk show host, author, tv producer, and philanthropist.

Her belief in the law of attraction began as she was

working as a host on *AM Chicago*. After reading *The Color Purple* and learning shortly after that it would be adapted for the big screen, she became obsessed. She told anyone who would listen and prayed fervently to God to have a role, no matter how small, in the movie. It wasn't long until Oprah was discovered by one of the producers, Quincy Jones and landed a major part. That role earned her various nominations for what was acclaimed as a breakout performance so she wasn't just in the movie, some might say she made the movie with her portrayal of the boisterous, brave and fierce Sophia.

Since that pivotal moment in her career, Oprah has gone on to transform viewers in countless ways. Most notably her work has caused us all to expand how we view this Universe and how we exist within it. She has curated conversations with the world's most recognized thought leaders, entertainers, and icons, one of which we'll discuss below.

Jim Carrey

The first time I heard Jim Carrey speak about how he manifested his way to success was one of my first experiences with the art of manifestation. During an interview with Oprah in 1997, he spoke about how he wrote himself a blank check for $10 million and just years later he was cast in his first major role in the movie Dumb and Dumber where he earned that exact amount. Since then, as you well know, he has gone on to become an actor who has brought the world many laughs across many screens. Outside of his profound abilities as an actor, he has also become a major source of inspiration over the years just by sharing his journey. Jim Carrey is no different than you nor is his ability to manifest any more powerful than what you also have access to. Take his story as an example of how you can connect to your desires and magnetize yourself to draw them right into your life.

Drake

What does our favorite Canadian rapper have to do with manifestation, you ask? The answer is plenty. Drake has spoken about the power of manifestation and visualization over the years.

During an interview on Rap Radar, he broke the recipe for his success down quite simply. He explained that directed, repetitive speech has allowed him to successfully manifest his current experience.

As you've learned through some of the practices explained in this book, your words and thoughts are things. As you wield them, you become a powerful creator of your own reality based on what you predominantly think about. Drake also goes on to acknowledge at one point in the interview that despite his incredible work ethic, there has also been a powerful source working behind the scenes in conjunction with his own efforts (co-creation).

People make the mistake of assuming that those who see the most success have a special set of instructions they have been given access to which no one else has. This couldn't be further from the truth. The question is can you get clear enough about what you want and develop the same consistency that Drake employed to bring him to his present day status?

Conor McGregor

When you hear the Irish mixed martial artist speak about his manifestation journey, it becomes clear what his recipe to success was: clarity, precision, and consistency. As a UFC lightweight and featherweight champion, Conor McGregor openly speaks about his personal journey with visualization.

He faced skepticism and doubt from family and friends as he worked towards a vision that had already played out in his mind countless times. That's why he had no doubt that eventually his efforts would pay off. Like most of us, Conor's visualization practice began as an early child where he would see himself in big stadiums surrounded by cheering fans.

That ability stayed with him through the years of building his career and remains with him now, even as an internationally recognized athlete. He's even used visualization techniques to script out the scenes and movements of fights before they take place! The greatest lesson we can learn from this powerful manifester is to stay committed to what we are working towards, even if no one around us understands. How you see yourself and what you see for yourself matters more than anything.

Everyone else will get on board once you've made things happen. There's no need to feel resentment about this. People just cannot see what was not meant for them to see. Accept that and keep moving forward.

Allyson Felix

As the most decorated American track and field athlete in the United States, with nine olympic medals and 13 world championship medals, it should come as no surprise that Allyson Felix incorporates visualization as a component in her training strategies. She understands that she has a limited window in which to make her efforts worthwhile as an Olympic athlete, so she must approach her process with precision. Part of this entails her running through mental images of what she considers to be a perfect race. Not only does this practice give her an opportunity to rehearse before bringing her talents to an international stage, but it also builds a level of confidence in what the future holds.

This strategy has served her well in the last five Olympic games that she has competed in. Perhaps she has also employed this powerful technique as she has expanded into entrepreneurship, motherhood and advocacy for women's health.

Lady Gaga

Since she landed on the pop scene with her debut single, "Just Dance", Lady Gaga has been a cultural phenomenon and source of inspiration for many. Her authenticity has been a major part of her success along with her powerful mindset.

Long before Stefani Germanotta became Lady Gaga, she already considered herself to be a star. Her fame began in her mind and was held with such conviction that the Universe brought that exact reality to her. In fact, she believes that this magic resides in each of us. "You have the freedom to pull the superstar out of yourself that you were born to be," she explained during a *60 Minutes* interview with Anderson Cooper in 2011.

These words are a nod to our internal force as eternal beings and expressions of the infinite. What Gaga is referring to is a power that each of us possess, but few successfully harness. Of course this is not due to a shortage of ability, but rather a failure to tap into the knowledge that reinforces our own divinity.

Gaga talks openly about her technique of telling herself lies (aka affirmations) until they become true. She understood that when a statement is repeated enough times with enough belief, eventually that vision must merge with reality.

Consider the language that you use (both externally and internally) and whether it builds up or strips away your power. The language we use will cultivate a mindset that serves as a canvas for what we are manifesting.

Russ

Singer, producer and rapper Russ says that the entire creation process for him is an act of manifestation. When you think of the concept of manifestation it makes perfect sense because as a musician you are essentially tapping into information that may not have been accessed by anyone on this plane. I firmly believe that all great ideas that have been realized were once themselves entities that existed in the non-physical world until a vessel successfully actualized them. So this process of bringing an idea through you, that did not exist before in this reality is 100% the finest example of manifestation.

From the time he was 17, Russ committed to his vision of being a successful musician and through affirmations, persistence, strong belief and a dash of delusion, he was able to successfully bring about that reality.

What I love about Russ's story is that he wasn't an overnight success. He was 11 projects in before he really started to be recognized in the industry to the level he is now. This is important because what many people don't realize when they begin to manifest is that timelines look different for everyone based on a number of factors - how consistent you are, how faithful you are, how specific you are, and how you feel from day to day.

It is no small undertaking to maintain faith in that space of time between when your vision exists in your mind and when it exists in real life. It can be easy to lose faith when people around you do (or when they don't have it in the first place), but it's important to remember that no one has the vision you've been gifted with. It's unique to you! During this time, you have to become an expert at experiencing an event internally before reality catches up. When reality does finally coincide with your vision, it will come as no surprise, because you've been preparing all along.

Israel Adesanya

"Everything comes from the imagination," says Nigeria-born, New Zealand-raised middleweight UFC champion, Israel Adesanya. Israel understands what many people fail to recognize - that everything which exists in this physical realm has a mental origin. One might even say that all great ideas have a spiritual origin and people serve as vessels for them to manifest through.

What manifested through Israel was his champion mindset, far before he had the accolades to reference himself as such. He used positive affirmations to speak his reality into existence and paired that belief with focused action.

During a post *UFC 287* interview Israel explained "I just want to show people the power of the human mind, the human spirit, what you can do, no matter what."

Israel's success is a story more than 15 years in the making, which is extremely important to highlight. Though he utilizes manifestation techniques in his life, that can never be a substitute for physical effort. Manifestation is most effective when paired with action.

Let's Manifest Magic

Now that you are better acquainted with the concept of manifestation, the ideas that lie behind it and even how people have successfully implemented it within their lives, it's time to start putting into practice what you've learned. The rest of this journal contains guided steps based on those outlined in this introduction. You can reference them at any time in your journey.

Start by identifying one thing that you are manifesting. Be clear and be specific!

She Manifests More

A GUIDED MANIFESTATION JOURNAL

A manifestation journal for _____

(name)

How To Use This Guided Journal

This is the beginning of a very special practice that you can take with you anywhere and use to manifest anything you desire. As you begin to incorporate this age old art form into your everyday, you'll want to reference the introduction.

Although the entire introduction will be of use to you as you are learning and developing your gifts, the "Steps to Manifest" section will be of extreme importance.

As you are going through the steps, you may want to read through the appropriate section to give yourself a refresher.

This guided journal is broken down into 4 parts:

- **Manifestation Steps**, to assist you through the process
- **Reflections**, to consider major learnings from your experience
- **Notes**, for anything else you would like to record
- **Things I Manifested**, your running log of your actualized desires

The first three segments, _Manifestation Steps_, _Reflections_, _and Notes_ – repeat throughout the journal to give you a holistic approach to each new manifestation "project" you take on.

The _Things I Manifested_ segment can be found at the back of your journal. May this tool bring you greater clarity, success and abundance in all forms! Happy Manifesting!

Identify Your Desire

Begin your manifestation journey by focusing on one thing you would like to manifest.

Get Specific

List out the details of your manifestation (the more the better). This will help you develop clarity.

Be Consistent

 **3.** Develop a plan for how you can regularly interact with your manifestation.

Create A Vessel

 **4.** Describe what you will use as a physical embodiment of your manifestation. Then create it!

Name Your Emotions

Think of how you will feel when experiencing your manifestation. Do your best to capture that.

Feel Your Emotions

What activities allow you to experience these emotions? Write them down below.

Show Up Today

 **7.** How does the version of you that has successfully manifested your desire walk through the world?

Harness Water

 **8.** How will you work with the power of water to support your goals?

Visualize Daily

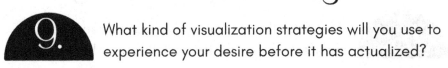

9. What kind of visualization strategies will you use to experience your desire before it has actualized?

Date Created:

Date Actualized:

Reflections

What have been some of your biggest challenges and hurdles?

What would you say are your biggest lessons learned?

Reflections

List anyone who inspired you to keep going in this process and how they did.

Are there any superpowers you unlocked that you were not aware of?

Notes

Notes

Notes

Notes

Notes

Notes

Identify Your Desire

Begin your manifestation journey by focusing on one thing you would like to manifest.

Get Specific

List out the details of your manifestation (the more the better). This will help you develop clarity.

Be Consistent

Develop a plan for how you can regularly interact with your manifestation.

Create A Vessel

Describe what you will use as a physical embodiment of your manifestation. Then create it!

Name Your Emotions

Think of how you will feel when experiencing your manifestation. Do your best to capture that.

Feel Your Emotions

What activities allow you to experience these emotions? Write them down below.

Show Up Today

How does the version of you that has successfully manifested your desire walk through the world?

Harness Water

How will you work with the power of water to support your goals?

Visualize Daily

9. What kind of visualization strategies will you use to experience your desire before it has actualized?

Date Created:

Date Actualized:

Reflections

What have been some of your biggest challenges and hurdles?

What would you say are your biggest lessons learned?

Reflections

List anyone who inspired you to keep
going in this process and how they did.

Are there any superpowers you
unlocked that you were not aware of?

Notes

Notes

Notes

Notes

Notes

Notes

Identify Your Desire

 Begin your manifestation journey by focusing on one thing you would like to manifest.

Get Specific

 List out the details of your manifestation (the more the better). This will help you develop clarity.

Be Consistent

Develop a plan for how you can regularly interact with your manifestation.

Create A Vessel

Describe what you will use as a physical embodiment of your manifestation. Then create it!

Name Your Emotions

Think of how you will feel when experiencing your manifestation. Do your best to capture that.

Feel Your Emotions

What activities allow you to experience these emotions? Write them down below.

Show Up Today

 How does the version of you that has successfully manifested your desire walk through the world?

Harness Water

 How will you work with the power of water to support your goals?

Visualize Daily

9. What kind of visualization strategies will you use to experience your desire before it has actualized?

Date Created:

Date Actualized:

Reflections

What have been some of your biggest challenges and hurdles?

What would you say are your biggest lessons learned?

Reflections

List anyone who inspired you to keep going in this process and how they did.

Are there any superpowers you unlocked that you were not aware of?

Notes

Notes

Notes

Notes

Notes

Notes

Identify Your Desire

Begin your manifestation journey by focusing on one thing you would like to manifest.

Get Specific

List out the details of your manifestation (the more the better). This will help you develop clarity.

Be Consistent

Develop a plan for how you can regularly interact with your manifestation.

Create A Vessel

Describe what you will use as a physical embodiment of your manifestation. Then create it!

Name Your Emotions

Think of how you will feel when experiencing your manifestation. Do your best to capture that.

Feel Your Emotions

What activities allow you to experience these emotions? Write them down below.

Show Up Today

 How does the version of you that has successfully manifested your desire walk through the world?

Harness Water

 How will you work with the power of water to support your goals?

Visualize Daily

9. What kind of visualization strategies will you use to experience your desire before it has actualized?

Date Created:

Date Actualized:

Reflections

What have been some of your biggest challenges and hurdles?

What would you say are your biggest lessons learned?

Reflections

List anyone who inspired you to keep going in this process and how they did.

Are there any superpowers you unlocked that you were not aware of?

Notes

Notes

Notes

Notes

Notes

Notes

Identify Your Desire

Begin your manifestation journey by focusing on one thing you would like to manifest.

Get Specific

List out the details of your manifestation (the more the better). This will help you develop clarity.

Be Consistent

3. Develop a plan for how you can regularly interact with your manifestation.

Create A Vessel

4. Describe what you will use as a physical embodiment of your manifestation. Then create it!

Name Your Emotions

5. Think of how you will feel when experiencing your manifestation. Do your best to capture that.

Feel Your Emotions

6. What activities allow you to experience these emotions? Write them down below.

Show Up Today

7. How does the version of you that has successfully manifested your desire walk through the world?

Harness Water

8. How will you work with the power of water to support your goals?

Visualize Daily

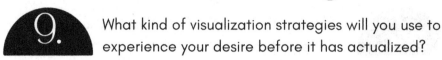

9. What kind of visualization strategies will you use to experience your desire before it has actualized?

Date Created:

Date Actualized:

Reflections

What have been some of your biggest
challenges and hurdles?

What would you say are your biggest
lessons learned?

Reflections

List anyone who inspired you to keep going in this process and how they did.

Are there any superpowers you unlocked that you were not aware of?

Notes

Notes

Notes

Notes

Notes

Notes

Identify Your Desire

 Begin your manifestation journey by focusing on one thing you would like to manifest.

Get Specific

 List out the details of your manifestation (the more the better). This will help you develop clarity.

Be Consistent

Develop a plan for how you can regularly interact with your manifestation.

Create A Vessel

Describe what you will use as a physical embodiment of your manifestation. Then create it!

Name Your Emotions

 Think of how you will feel when experiencing your manifestation. Do your best to capture that.

Feel Your Emotions

 What activities allow you to experience these emotions? Write them down below.

Show Up Today

How does the version of you that has successfully manifested your desire walk through the world?

Harness Water

How will you work with the power of water to support your goals?

Visualize Daily

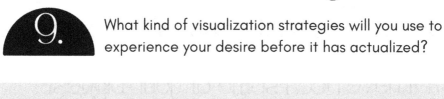

9. What kind of visualization strategies will you use to experience your desire before it has actualized?

Date Created:

Date Actualized:

Reflections

What have been some of your biggest
challenges and hurdles?

What would you say are your biggest
lessons learned?

Reflections

List anyone who inspired you to keep going in this process and how they did.

Are there any superpowers you unlocked that you were not aware of?

Notes

Notes

Notes

Notes

Notes

Notes

Identify Your Desire

Begin your manifestation journey by focusing on one thing you would like to manifest.

Get Specific

List out the details of your manifestation (the more the better). This will help you develop clarity.

Be Consistent

Develop a plan for how you can regularly interact with your manifestation.

Create A Vessel

Describe what you will use as a physical embodiment of your manifestation. Then create it!

Name Your Emotions

Think of how you will feel when experiencing your manifestation. Do your best to capture that.

Feel Your Emotions

What activities allow you to experience these emotions? Write them down below.

Show Up Today

 How does the version of you that has successfully
manifested your desire walk through the world?

Harness Water

 How will you work with the power of water to
support your goals?

Visualize Daily

9. What kind of visualization strategies will you use to experience your desire before it has actualized?

Date Created:

Date Actualized:

Reflections

What have been some of your biggest challenges and hurdles?

What would you say are your biggest lessons learned?

Reflections

List anyone who inspired you to keep going in this process and how they did.

Are there any superpowers you unlocked that you were not aware of?

Notes

Notes

Notes

Notes

Notes

Notes

Identify Your Desire

 Begin your manifestation journey by focusing on one thing you would like to manifest.

Get Specific

 List out the details of your manifestation (the more the better). This will help you develop clarity.

Be Consistent

 Develop a plan for how you can regularly interact with your manifestation.

Create A Vessel

 Describe what you will use as a physical embodiment of your manifestation. Then create it!

Name Your Emotions

Think of how you will feel when experiencing your manifestation. Do your best to capture that.

Feel Your Emotions

What activities allow you to experience these emotions? Write them down below.

Show Up Today

 **7.** How does the version of you that has successfully manifested your desire walk through the world?

Harness Water

 **8.** How will you work with the power of water to support your goals?

Visualize Daily

9. What kind of visualization strategies will you use to experience your desire before it has actualized?

Date Created:

Date Actualized:

Reflections

What have been some of your biggest challenges and hurdles?

What would you say are your biggest lessons learned?

Reflections

List anyone who inspired you to keep going in this process and how they did.

Are there any superpowers you unlocked that you were not aware of?

Notes

Notes

Notes

Notes

Notes

Notes

Identify Your Desire

Begin your manifestation journey by focusing on one thing you would like to manifest.

Get Specific

List out the details of your manifestation (the more the better). This will help you develop clarity.

Be Consistent

Develop a plan for how you can regularly interact with your manifestation.

Create A Vessel

Describe what you will use as a physical embodiment of your manifestation. Then create it!

Name Your Emotions

Think of how you will feel when experiencing your manifestation. Do your best to capture that.

Feel Your Emotions

What activities allow you to experience these emotions? Write them down below.

Show Up Today

 How does the version of you that has successfully manifested your desire walk through the world?

Harness Water

 How will you work with the power of water to support your goals?

Visualize Daily

9. What kind of visualization strategies will you use to experience your desire before it has actualized?

Date Created:

Date Actualized:

Reflections

What have been some of your biggest challenges and hurdles?

What would you say are your biggest lessons learned?

Reflections

List anyone who inspired you to keep going in this process and how they did.

Are there any superpowers you unlocked that you were not aware of?

Notes

Notes

Notes

Notes

Notes

Notes

Identify Your Desire

 Begin your manifestation journey by focusing on one thing you would like to manifest.

Get Specific

 List out the details of your manifestation (the more the better). This will help you develop clarity.

Be Consistent

Develop a plan for how you can regularly interact with your manifestation.

Create A Vessel

Describe what you will use as a physical embodiment of your manifestation. Then create it!

Name Your Emotions

Think of how you will feel when experiencing your manifestation. Do your best to capture that.

Feel Your Emotions

What activities allow you to experience these emotions? Write them down below.

Show Up Today

How does the version of you that has successfully manifested your desire walk through the world?

Harness Water

How will you work with the power of water to support your goals?

Visualize Daily

 **9.** What kind of visualization strategies will you use to experience your desire before it has actualized?

Date Created:

Date Actualized:

Reflections

What have been some of your biggest challenges and hurdles?

What would you say are your biggest lessons learned?

Reflections

List anyone who inspired you to keep going in this process and how they did.

Are there any superpowers you unlocked that you were not aware of?

Notes

Notes

Notes

Notes

Notes

Notes

Identify Your Desire

 Begin your manifestation journey by focusing on one thing you would like to manifest.

Get Specific

 List out the details of your manifestation (the more the better). This will help you develop clarity.

Be Consistent

 **3.** Develop a plan for how you can regularly interact with your manifestation.

Create A Vessel

 **4.** Describe what you will use as a physical embodiment of your manifestation. Then create it!

Name Your Emotions

Think of how you will feel when experiencing your manifestation. Do your best to capture that.

Feel Your Emotions

What activities allow you to experience these emotions? Write them down below.

Show Up Today

7. How does the version of you that has successfully manifested your desire walk through the world?

Harness Water

8. How will you work with the power of water to support your goals?

Visualize Daily

9. What kind of visualization strategies will you use to experience your desire before it has actualized?

Date Created:

Date Actualized:

Reflections

What have been some of your biggest challenges and hurdles?

What would you say are your biggest lessons learned?

Reflections

List anyone who inspired you to keep going in this process and how they did.

Are there any superpowers you unlocked that you were not aware of?

Notes

Notes

Notes

Notes

Notes

Notes

Identify Your Desire

 Begin your manifestation journey by focusing on one thing you would like to manifest.

Get Specific

 List out the details of your manifestation (the more the better). This will help you develop clarity.

Be Consistent

Develop a plan for how you can regularly interact with your manifestation.

Create A Vessel

Describe what you will use as a physical embodiment of your manifestation. Then create it!

Name Your Emotions

Think of how you will feel when experiencing your manifestation. Do your best to capture that.

Feel Your Emotions

What activities allow you to experience these emotions? Write them down below.

Show Up Today

7. How does the version of you that has successfully manifested your desire walk through the world?

Harness Water

8. How will you work with the power of water to support your goals?

Visualize Daily

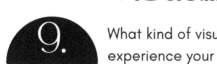 What kind of visualization strategies will you use to experience your desire before it has actualized?

Date Created:

Date Actualized:

Reflections

What have been some of your biggest challenges and hurdles?

What would you say are your biggest lessons learned?

Reflections

List anyone who inspired you to keep
going in this process and how they did.

Are there any superpowers you
unlocked that you were not aware of?

Notes

Notes

Notes

Notes

Notes

Notes

Identify Your Desire

Begin your manifestation journey by focusing on one thing you would like to manifest.

Get Specific

List out the details of your manifestation (the more the better). This will help you develop clarity.

Be Consistent

 Develop a plan for how you can regularly interact with your manifestation.

Create A Vessel

 Describe what you will use as a physical embodiment of your manifestation. Then create it!

Name Your Emotions

5. Think of how you will feel when experiencing your manifestation. Do your best to capture that.

Feel Your Emotions

6. What activities allow you to experience these emotions? Write them down below.

Show Up Today

How does the version of you that has successfully manifested your desire walk through the world?

Harness Water

How will you work with the power of water to support your goals?

Visualize Daily

9. What kind of visualization strategies will you use to experience your desire before it has actualized?

Date Created:

Date Actualized:

Reflections

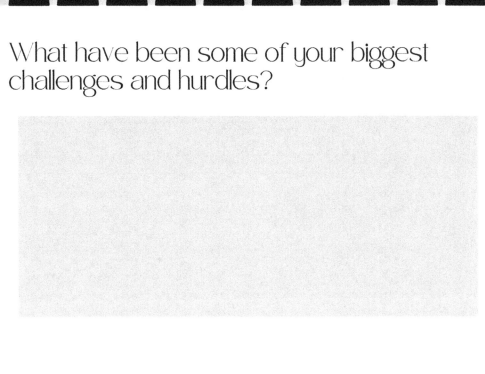

What have been some of your biggest challenges and hurdles?

What would you say are your biggest lessons learned?

Reflections

List anyone who inspired you to keep going in this process and how they did.

Are there any superpowers you unlocked that you were not aware of?

Notes

Notes

Notes

Notes

Notes

Notes

Identify Your Desire

Begin your manifestation journey by focusing on one thing you would like to manifest.

Get Specific

List out the details of your manifestation (the more the better). This will help you develop clarity.

Be Consistent

Develop a plan for how you can regularly interact with your manifestation.

Create A Vessel

Describe what you will use as a physical embodiment of your manifestation. Then create it!

Name Your Emotions

Think of how you will feel when experiencing your manifestation. Do your best to capture that.

Feel Your Emotions

What activities allow you to experience these emotions? Write them down below.

Show Up Today

How does the version of you that has successfully manifested your desire walk through the world?

Harness Water

How will you work with the power of water to support your goals?

Visualize Daily

9. What kind of visualization strategies will you use to experience your desire before it has actualized?

Date Created:

Date Actualized:

Reflections

What have been some of your biggest challenges and hurdles?

What would you say are your biggest lessons learned?

Reflections

List anyone who inspired you to keep going in this process and how they did.

Are there any superpowers you unlocked that you were not aware of?

Notes

Notes

Notes

Notes

Notes

Notes

Identify Your Desire

 Begin your manifestation journey by focusing on one thing you would like to manifest.

Get Specific

 List out the details of your manifestation (the more the better). This will help you develop clarity.

Be Consistent

Develop a plan for how you can regularly interact with your manifestation.

Create A Vessel

Describe what you will use as a physical embodiment of your manifestation. Then create it!

Name Your Emotions

Think of how you will feel when experiencing your manifestation. Do your best to capture that.

Feel Your Emotions

What activities allow you to experience these emotions? Write them down below.

Show Up Today

 How does the version of you that has successfully manifested your desire walk through the world?

Harness Water

 How will you work with the power of water to support your goals?

Visualize Daily

9. What kind of visualization strategies will you use to experience your desire before it has actualized?

Date Created:

Date Actualized:

Reflections

What have been some of your biggest challenges and hurdles?

What would you say are your biggest lessons learned?

Reflections

List anyone who inspired you to keep going in this process and how they did.

Are there any superpowers you unlocked that you were not aware of?

Notes

Notes

Notes

Notes

Notes

Notes

Identify Your Desire

Begin your manifestation journey by focusing on one thing you would like to manifest.

Get Specific

List out the details of your manifestation (the more the better). This will help you develop clarity.

Be Consistent

Develop a plan for how you can regularly interact with your manifestation.

Create A Vessel

Describe what you will use as a physical embodiment of your manifestation. Then create it!

Name Your Emotions

Think of how you will feel when experiencing your manifestation. Do your best to capture that.

Feel Your Emotions

What activities allow you to experience these emotions? Write them down below.

Show Up Today

 How does the version of you that has successfully
manifested your desire walk through the world?

Harness Water

 How will you work with the power of water to
support your goals?

Visualize Daily

9. What kind of visualization strategies will you use to experience your desire before it has actualized?

Date Created:

Date Actualized:

Reflections

What have been some of your biggest challenges and hurdles?

What would you say are your biggest lessons learned?

Reflections

List anyone who inspired you to keep going in this process and how they did.

Are there any superpowers you unlocked that you were not aware of?

Notes

Notes

Notes

Notes

Notes

Notes

Identify Your Desire

Begin your manifestation journey by focusing on one thing you would like to manifest.

Get Specific

List out the details of your manifestation (the more the better). This will help you develop clarity.

Be Consistent

Develop a plan for how you can regularly interact with your manifestation.

Create A Vessel

Describe what you will use as a physical embodiment of your manifestation. Then create it!

Name Your Emotions

Think of how you will feel when experiencing your manifestation. Do your best to capture that.

Feel Your Emotions

What activities allow you to experience these emotions? Write them down below.

Show Up Today

7. How does the version of you that has successfully manifested your desire walk through the world?

Harness Water

8. How will you work with the power of water to support your goals?

Visualize Daily

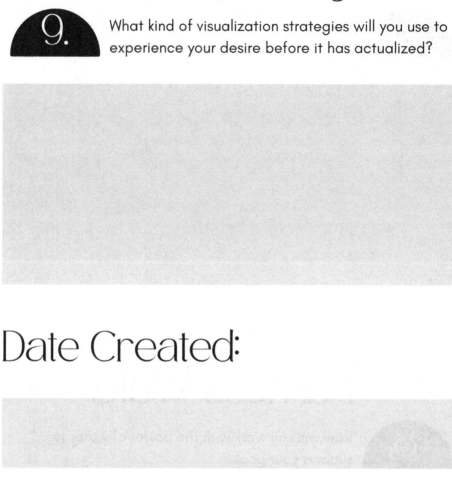

9. What kind of visualization strategies will you use to experience your desire before it has actualized?

Date Created:

Date Actualized:

Reflections

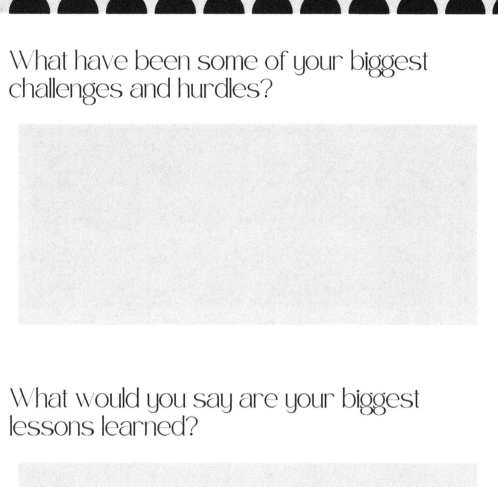

What have been some of your biggest challenges and hurdles?

What would you say are your biggest lessons learned?

Reflections

List anyone who inspired you to keep going in this process and how they did.

Are there any superpowers you unlocked that you were not aware of?

Notes

Notes

Notes

Notes

Notes

Notes

Identify Your Desire

 Begin your manifestation journey by focusing on one thing you would like to manifest.

Get Specific

 List out the details of your manifestation (the more the better). This will help you develop clarity.

Be Consistent

 Develop a plan for how you can regularly interact with your manifestation.

Create A Vessel

 Describe what you will use as a physical embodiment of your manifestation. Then create it!

Name Your Emotions

Think of how you will feel when experiencing your manifestation. Do your best to capture that.

Feel Your Emotions

What activities allow you to experience these emotions? Write them down below.

Show Up Today

7. How does the version of you that has successfully manifested your desire walk through the world?

Harness Water

8. How will you work with the power of water to support your goals?

Visualize Daily

 **9.** What kind of visualization strategies will you use to experience your desire before it has actualized?

Date Created:

Date Actualized:

Reflections

What have been some of your biggest challenges and hurdles?

What would you say are your biggest lessons learned?

Reflections

List anyone who inspired you to keep
going in this process and how they did.

Are there any superpowers you
unlocked that you were not aware of?

Notes

Notes

Notes

Notes

Notes

Notes

Things I Manifested

What	Date

Things I Manifested

What	Date

Resources

"A Day in Dublin With Conor McGregor." YouTube, uploaded by MMAFightingonSBN, 8 November, 2016, https://youtu.be/JcUE6Nwx3EE

Beretta, Leonardo. (2018). Nikola Tesla and the 369 Code: Decoding God's Thumbprint. CreateSpace Independent Publishing Platform.

Dugan, Ellen and Eilidh Grove, et al. (2014). Llewellyn's 2015 Magical Almanac: Practical Magic For Everyday Living. Llewellyn Publications.

Hicks, Esther and Jerry Hicks. (2004). Ask and It Is Given. Hay House Inc.

Goddard, Neville. (2023). Feeling Is The Secret.

Goswami, Richa. (2021, November 21). Visualization: Allyson Felix Reveals This Training Mindset Helped Her Stay Competitive at 36 Years, Essentially Sports. https://www.essentiallysports.com/visualization-allyson-felix-reveals-this-training-mindset-helped-her-stay-competitive-at-36-years-us-sports-news-allyson-felix/

"Israel Adesanya Post-Fight Press Conference | UFC 287" YouTube, uploaded by UFC - Ultimate Fighting Championship, 9 April 2023, https://youtu.be/8wyM6obrAAo

"Israel Adesanya Mindset for Success." YouTube, uploaded by BoxTalk TV, 14 May 2020, https://youtu.be/0uMlkf0wRgU

"Israel Adesanya's Thoughts On Manifestation." YouTube, uploaded by New Mentalities, 18 July 2022, https://youtube.com/shorts/buFfiQnu5uA?feature=share

Jean-Philippe, McKenzie. (2021, September 14). Allyson Felix Is History's Most Decorated Olympic Track & Field Athlete, Oprah Daily. https://www.oprahdaily.com/life/a29518464/who-is-allyson-felix/

Kawatra, Pallavi and Rathai Rajagopalan 2015. 'Cinnamon: Mystic powers of a minute ingredient', Pharmacognosy Research, vol. 7, S1-6.

"Lady Gaga Gives CNN Her Unique Recipe for Success." YouTube, uploaded by WORLDNEWS, 17 September 2009, https://youtu.be/vFGchzvu41k

"Lady Gaga & The Art of Fame." Interview by Anderson Cooper. YouTube, uploaded by CBS News, 13 February 2011, https://www.youtube.com/watch?v=SBk22UhcJlo

Larson, Christian D. (2008). Your Forces And How To Use Them.

Miller, Brian B.Dot and Elliott Wilson, hosts. "Drake". Rap Radar, Episode 84, 25 December 2019, https://rapradar.com/features/rap-radar-podcast-drake/

Murphy, Dr. Joseph D (1963). The Power of Your Subconscious Mind. Prentice-Hall, Inc.

"The Mysterious Power of Three", Ancient Aliens, Season 6, Episode 1, YouTube, uploaded by History Channel, 25 October 2022, https://www.youtube.com/watch?v=kxVXDG5UO3g

"The Mystical Secrets Of Water", uploaded by Sadhguru, 22 March, 2019, https://www.youtube.com/watch?v=1kKGzCL4D5w